THE PRINCE VIJAYA PALA OF CEYLON

1634-1654

THE PRINCE VIJAYA PALA OF CEYLON

1634-1654

FROM THE ORIGINAL DOCUMENTS AT LISBON

P. E. PIERIS

GYAN

Published by

Gyan Publishing House
5, Ansari Road
Daryaganj, New Delhi-110002
Phone: 011-47034999, 9811692060
E-mail: books@gyanbooks.com

Distribution Network
gyanbooks.com
India, USA, Canada, UK, Australia, France

ISBN : 978-81-212-3921-9 (PB)
First Published, Colombo, 1928

2nd Impression 2020

Printed at: Gyan Press, Delhi.

The
Prince Vijaya Pala of Ceylon
1634-1654
Author: P. E. Pieris

THE

PRINCE VIJAYA PALA OF CEYLON

1634-1654

from the original documents at Lisbon

BY

P. E. PIERIS,

DERANIYAGALA SAMARASINHA SRIWARDHANA,

Litt. D. (Cantab.), Socio do Instituto de Coimbra.

COLOMBO:

PRINTED AT THE C.A.C. PRESS.

1927.

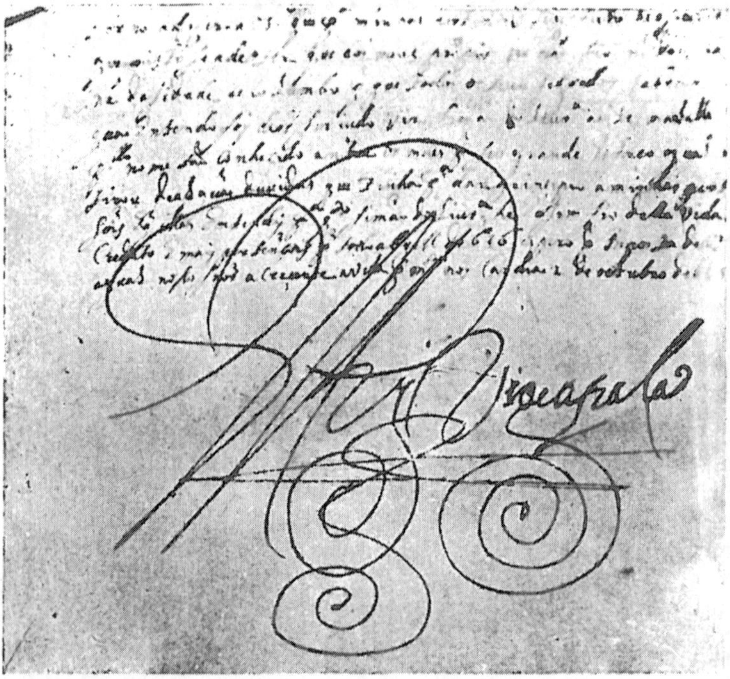

SIGNATURE OF VIJAYA PALA.

INDEX.

INDEX

Page

PREFACE.

In this little book I have put together such information, hitherto unpublished, as I was able to collect during a recent visit to Portugal, regarding Vijaya Pala, brother of Raja Sinha, King of Ceylon. A couple of documents from the Archives at the Hague, the translations of which were courteously placed at my disposal by the authorities at the India Office, as well as the rare Pamphlet dealing with the Prince's baptism, which was traced by Fräulein Fitzler at Evora, are also included. There are interesting details about the Prince in the *Jornada do Reino de Huva* at the Biblioteca da Ajuda, but these have been excluded as they are largely reproduced in Fernão de Queiroz's *Conquista de Ceylão.*

The original documents will be published in the Series which is in course of preparation, if the necessary funds are forthcoming.

I have gratefully to acknowledge the assistance which I have received from the officials of the Archivo Nacional da Torre do Tombo at Lisbon, and of the Biblioteca da Evora, and from Fräulein Fitzler by whom my translations were revised.

To that New Spirit, which has inspired the Training Colony at Peradeniya, I offer this.

INTRODUCTION

A treaty[1] which was signed on the second of July, 1617, between the Portuguese and Senevirat, the gentle and cultured Prince, once a priest, who occupied the Sinhalese throne, restored some semblance of peace in Ceylon, which for so many years had been exposed to a peculiarly ruthless and desolating warfare. The King's three sons—Kumara Sinha, Vijaya Pala, and Maha Astana—were still of tender age, the youngest not being above five years, and his great anxiety was to secure a chance of educating them, unharassed by hostilities which drove him from one place of hiding to another. The Portuguese, however, cherished different views ; they were determined to bring the whole of the Island under their flag, and the interval of peace only served for developing their plans. Accordingly in 1624 and 1626 they boldly occupied portions of the King's territory and erected on his Eastern coast, two forts[2] which cut off his communications with India on that side.

It was clear that war could not be avoided much longer, and in 1628 the King proceeded to divide his Kingdom among his sons. Uva, with its great highland plains, was allotted to the eldest, and Matale to Vijaya Pala; while the Kanda Uda Rata—the Country above the Mountains—the original principality which Europeans have named Kandy, and from which the Kingdom came into existence, was reserved for the youngest of the three, Maha Astana.

The war which now began was marked by devastating raids on the side of the Portuguese, and the skilful guerilla tactics of the Sinhalese, which resulted in the invading army and its Captain-General, Constantino de Sa y Noronha, being destroyed in September, 1630. The young Princes bore themselves well in this fight :—

" With the hosts of Uva Tunkinda and Matale, right gallantly did the Princely pair carry themselves through this Red Sea of blood. Parangi Padres, doughty Capitans, the Tuppasi host, and Kustantinu de Sa, were there encircled and cut to pieces. Thus was the battle fought."

That is how the most spirited poem in the Sinhalese language, the *Parangi Hatane*, the Story of the Feringhis, concludes its description of the sanguinary conflict[3].

The military leadership was now entrusted to the three brothers and it was only after a hard struggle that the Portuguese were able to avoid the total destruction of their hold on the country, till in 1634 a fresh treaty was entered into[4] But it was not the intention of the Portuguese that this should put an end to their policy of conquest. They knew that Vijaya Pala was friendly towards them and that he was aggrieved at the subordinate position which had been assigned to him. "The Kingdom of Candia belongs to me as the elder brother" he asserted (Doct. 1). They hoped that he would prove a valuable tool for destroying the power of the Sinhalese by creating internal discord, in accordance with the policy which Dom Affonço de Noronha[5] had enunciated in 1552 and which other Europeans subsequently adopted. The Conde de Linhares had already sent him tempting offers to secure for him the throne with Portuguese arms, and de Sa acting on the Viceroy's behalf, had repeatedly pressed the offer, at the same time undertaking to give him the Seven Korales, which was under Portuguese control, till such time as the Kingdom could be subdued. Their successors continued the same line of action, while the death of Kumarasinha which occurred in 1634 and the events which followed, increased the attraction of their proposals. Vijaya Pala considered himself the lawful heir to the fief of Uva and to all the late Prince's treasures, but Maha Astana, as Aga Raja, insisted on resuming the former, and allowed his brother only a share out of the latter. (D. 1)

Vijaya Pala in spite of his intense irritation, was powerless to resist, and on the 10th of October, 1634, he addressed a confidential letter to the Viceroy asking for a safe conduct to enable him to join the Portuguese (D. 1). This was entrusted to a Portuguese, Symão de Oliveyra, and was followed by a second letter dated the 2nd of October, 1635, Senevirat having died in the interval (D. 2). The Viceroy was delighted with the turn of affairs and instructed the Captain-General in Ceylon, Diogo de Mello de Castro, to encourage the Prince in his design and to get him within Portuguese territory, (D. 3), while his Council in ordering a safe conduct to be sent, directed the General to be ready to receive the Prince "for it is realised that this is the best method of reducing the Island under our authority" (D. 4). These measures were approved at Lisbon (D. 5), but to the Viceroy's disappointment they came to nothing "in consequence of the natural fickleness of this race and the little confidence which as a rule can be placed on it" as he explained (D. 6).

Some kind of reconciliation had apparently been effected between the brothers, and Vijaya Pala was back at Court. The attitude of the Portuguese, however, remained so unsatisfactory, that Raja Sinha, as Maha Astana was now called, entered into negotiations with the Hollanders at Batavia[6], and at his invitation two of their emissaries came to visit him in November, 1637. The Captain-General was greatly perturbed by this development, and again resorted to the old device of creating dissension between the brothers. The King, in order to mark his displeasure at the Captain-General's conduct, declined to receive any letters from him, and therefore the latter wrote to Vijaya Pala, complaining bitterly of the King's action in treating with the Hollanders. He described them as "subjects of and rebels against the King of Portugal, pirates well known in the whole of India, hated by all Indian potentates............Let the Dutch, who are called to drive us out of the Island, freely come: but I predict for this Kingdom ruin and trouble if they take our place........We are now at war." (D. 7).

Nor did he wait long; a further quarrel of a personal nature brought matters to a crisis, and in spite of the earnest remonstrances of his Council, he insisted on declaring war[7]. Every available fighting man was rapidly mustered, and in March, 1638, a great army commanded by the General in person crossed the frontier. The result was a terrible disaster; the Sinhalese attacked them on Palm Sunday, the 28th of March:

"Like the roar of ten thousand thunderbolts the cannon bellowed forth at once, shattering heaven and earth and the mountain tops, and we rushed into their midst, some laying about them with their clubs, some treading them underfoot or severing their necks at a single stroke, while others looked on at the sight from near," sang the writer of the *Parangi Hatane.* The killed were estimated at 2,500 and included the General and nearly all the Portuguese (Doc. 8).

This great victory, to which Vijaya Pala materially contributed, failed to cement his relations with his brother. His sympathies led to a surreptitious attempt on his part to set his prisoners at liberty. Fernão de

Mendoça, the most important of them, who had been known to Vijaya Pala when he was sent as an emissary by the Viceroy Pero da Silva Molle to seduce the Prince from his allegiance, was allowed to escape.[8] Raja Sinha was therefore compelled to have him placed under arrest, but once again a reconciliation was effected,[9] and Vijaya Pala was sent back to Matale (D. 12).

The intrigues of the Portuguese, however, did not cease in spite of Raja Sinha's protests. The new Captain-General, Dom Felipe Mascarenhas, reported that the quarrel between the brothers had become acute (D. 9) and the Viceroy hailed this as an act of God, from which important results could be expected (D. 10). Indeed the General went so far as to write to Raja Sinha on the 21st of December, 1640, threatening to displace him from the throne in favour of his brother[10]. But the Portuguese were in very serious straits, for already four of their strongholds, including Galle, the centre of the chief cinnamon yielding district, had been wrested from them. The fort at Mada Kalapuwa had been occupied by a garrison of Hollanders on behalf of the King: with their Captain the Prince opened negotiations, but received no encouragement (D. 11). About July, 1641, war broke out between the brothers in Uva. Vijaya Pala appeared in Sabaragamuwa and was urged by Mascarenhas to come and help him in Colombo, at the same time renewing the promise to give him the

Seven Korales till such time as the Kingdom could be subdued (D. 12, 19). Vijaya Pala thereupon marched down with 2,000 fighting men and a large suite, and was received with great distinctions.[11] A fleet of the Hollanders was at the time threatening the coast, and a few days after his arrival seven of their vessels which had been engaged in the blockade of Goa, appeared before Colombo.[12] The Portuguese were in consternation, and the Prince's men were a welcome addition to their forces, both in garrison and on the field, while he undertook the completion of the moat on the Mapane side of Colombo at his own expense (D. 19).

But the General, in spite of his fine promises, did nothing to assist Vijaya Pala to conquer his brother's kingdom, and friction soon arose. An armed encounter took place between the Prince's men and the Portuguese soldiers, and he found himself being treated as a prisoner. He thereupon tried to get into communication with the Hollanders: "I am now practically a prisoner of the Portuguese" he wrote in October, 1642, "and cannot stay here any longer......I am in a sad plight in this town of Columbo," which he described as "this frightful hell." Some of his letters were intercepted and Mascarenhas decided to remove him to Goa, and accordingly he went in person and transferred him to the Convent of S. Francisco within the Fort (D. 17). It would seem that when this was done much of the Prince's treasure was stolen. He was not long after shipped to Goa with great decorum and ceremony (D. 15), the Prince arriving there on the 26th of March, 1643.[13]

Six weeks later he addressed a letter to the Viceroy (D. 12) in which he set out his claims, his grievance at the treatment he had received from Mascarenhas, and his decision to accept Christianity on certain conditions which he specified. He demanded that he should be treated with the consideration due to his rank, that the treasure of which he declared he had been robbed should be restored to him, that he should be given the necessary help to conquer his brother's kingdom, and that he should be sent back to Ceylon for the purpose. This communication brought no relief, and the Prince appealed to King Dom João IV The ecclesiastics were his strong supporters, for royal converts were much desired. The Archbishop of Mira took a special interest in his case, and on his advice the Prince wrote to the Pope announcing his proposed conversion. Urbano VIII.'s congratulatory Brief, translated into Portuguese by the Archbishop, has been preserved (D. 13), and was dated under the Seal of the Fisherman on the 19th of March, 1644.

The King on his part referred the Prince's case to the Viceroy for report (D. 14), but the reply received from India (D. 15) was unfavourable. The Viceroy characterised the Prince as "evil and wicked," while pointing out that he had been provided with his reasonable expenses from the King's Fazenda. With the receipt of the Papal Brief Vijaya Pala decided to be baptised and asked Dom João to be his god-father: the latter consented and instructed the Viceroy to act on his behalf (D. 16). He again directed a strict inquiry into the Prince's complaints, but forbade his being sent back to Ceylon "because of the prejudice which his person and residence there will create." Nor should he be sent on to the Reino, on account of the expense this would involve.

By the time these orders reached India, Mascarenhas had succeeded as Viceroy and he wrote and explained the circumstances of the Prince's removal from Ceylon. The baptism took place on the 8th of December, 1646, in the Church of São Francisco at Goa, and a valuable and detailed account[14] of the incident has been preserved (D. 18). He was given the name of Dom Theodosio, and at the same time he was ceremoniously crowned by the Viceroy. The Prince communicated all this to his Royal god-father, who does not appear to have had much confidence in him, and ordered that he should be carefully watched and not allowed to leave the city pending further instructions (D. 20).

Vijaya Pala on his side wrote through his "Grand Chamberlain," a Sinhalese Prince who bore the name of Dom Duarte de Braganza, to Dom João, whom, apparently in view of his own coronation, he now regarded as a brother. He complained bitterly of the way in which he had been robbed by the Portuguese, so that he was now in poverty and unable properly to maintain a befitting household. He was heavily in debt and the allowance given to him from the Fazenda was not duly paid. He begged for the treatment he was entitled to expect, and, if it could be arranged, that he should be allowed to proceed to the Reino.

The Viceroy, however, reported that on an inquiry being held by the Inquisitor no evidence of the alleged robbery was forthcoming: he added "this King is very fantastic with little solidity in his affairs." (D. 21).

That Vijaya Pala had a substantial grievance is beyond doubt, and strong representations were made on his behalf by the Patriarch of Ethiopia among others (D. 22, 23). There were rumours that the Hollanders were trying to get him into their power for their own purposes, while Raja Sinha was detaining the Portuguese ambassadors who were sent to him, as security for the Prince's safety. The Viceroy reported on the 30th of November, 1650, that he was receiving an allowance of 250 xerafims a month, which the Viceroy considered a generous sum:[15] but the King ordered the amount to be increased, and this was done (D. 24). The Prince's appeal had some effect and in March, 1652, he wrote to his brother Raja Sinha a letter in the Tamil language, in which he informed him that instructions had been received to transfer him to Lisbon, if hostilities did not recur in Ceylon.[16] His death two years later prevented these instructions being carried out.[17] European ideas, badly digested, denationalized this well-meaning but shallow man, and ruined his life.

The following description of his personal appearance has been preserved by an eye-witness, Captain João Ribeiro :—

"He was dignified, modest, courteous, of a stately bearing, and appeared about thirty-four years old, slim of body and very erect. His long hair was curled at the ends, and his beard was worn in the Portuguese fashion, with a moustache which was not very full; his colour was like that of the quince, and he was always very cheerful and friendly with the Portuguese; but when he spoke with the natives, his bearing was royal, austere, and very stately."

The Archbishop of Mira considered him "a Prince of great parts, both natural and acquired, for besides being graceful there can be seen in his stature and bearing the Majesty worthy of an Empire........He is gifted with high courage and spirit........he is a great horseman, very skilled in all arts which become a Prince. He speaks Portuguese with much fluency and ease."

Certain aspects of his character were essentially Sinhalese. However sunk his fortunes he could never forget his royal birth: for social position in Ceylon as in India, is independent of worldly prosperity. He may be a prisoner in all but name, but he still calls himself "a lord of lords, a god of lords" (D. 11), for as Raja Sinha pointed out to the Hollanders,[18] it was not improper to attribute divinity to members of his family, just as was done in the case of the Roman

Emperors. His royal insignia and royal music accompany him on his journey (D. 12) and even as a pensioner at Goa, Princes and high noblemen are members of his suite (D. 19). He must be treated as the grandson of the Emperador, Dharmapala, on whose donation the King of Portugal founded his claims to the country (D. 12), and the state which he maintained should not be less than that provided for that ill-fated ruler (D. 19).

The King of Portugal is his "brother" and to pay for the men who were engaged on that King's service, the Prince pawned his own jewels. When he went to Colombo his intention was that his presence should give the Portuguese that courage and confidence which he thought they needed. His royal position must be manifest to all, and he would take no part in public functions till that was officially recognized (D. 19). The treatment he had received in Colombo had cast a slur on his dignity, and his desire was to return there so that the stain might be wiped away. If restored to his kingdom he is willing to enter into a treaty with the King of Portugal, but he will subscribe to nothing which will stain his honour or adversely affect his dignity.

Royalty must act in accordance with the *Dasa Raja Dharma*, the Ten Precepts for the guidance of Kings; and so the Prince is one "who speaks the truth." "I once gave my word to a Portuguese and kept it: why should I act differently towards you," he urges on the Hollanders. It is a royal duty to defend the helpless; therefore he "takes under his protection those who seek his aid." "I was the refuge of everyone in the many disasters the Portuguese suffered," he reminds them. A King should be open-handed, and so at Goa widows, maidens, orphans and poor and crippled soldados all turned to him in their distress, and not in vain. Even in dealing with a foe a King must be honourable. He had upbraided his own brother for what he considered his treacherous treatment of the Hollanders, and when the Portuguese suggested to him the poisoning of the garrison at Galle, he is deeply shocked; they must "not now expect that I should act the same part as I condemned in my brother." He is passionate, like most of his countrymen. In spite of his quarrel with his brother a letter shown to him by the Portuguese to the effect that Raja Sinha and the Prince of Orange would soon be prisoners in their hands, moved him to such a rage that he struck the messenger. In the eyes of the Portuguese the outbreaks of the Prince were "evil acts and wicked proceedings" and proofs of his "changeable and restless" nature (D. 15).

In some respects he was curiously shallow and Mascarenhas was right when he described him as "very fantastic with little solidity" (D. 21). Curiosities and western novelties pleased him, and even when war was close at hand he would write to the enemy's General about the arrival of a dealer in them from Goa (D. 7). As a Buddhist, his consideration for the religious feelings of others had not been lessened by the evil example set by the Portuguese, " whose images of God and your Lady and the Saints I ever treated with all veneration." (D. 12).

The education to which he was subjected, helped to accentuate all the weak points in his weak character. The dangers of a missionary influence which was directed by political considerations had revealed themselves from the start, in the time of Bhuwanaika Bahu, and the career of this Prince is a pathetic illustration of their result. Vikrama Bahu barely escaped. His feeble minded son Jaya Vira succumbed; and the latter's infant daughter Dona Catherina, the Prince's mother, was left to be moulded by their hands. Senevirat, with the liberality of mind and lack of foresight which Bhuwanaika Bahu had shown, allowed them the same intimate access to his Court. It was a source of gratification to the Queen when the youthful Vijaya Pala was entrusted to a Franciscan, the Frey Francisco Negrão (D. 1), and the consequences were curiously similar to what had attended the intimacy of Andre de Sousa and his Franciscan friends with King Bhuwanaika Bahu's Queen a hundred years before. " I state, Senhor, that I was born with a strong predilection for the Portuguese nation " wrote Vijaya Pala. " In my earliest years, greatly to the satisfaction of the Queen my mother, there was assigned to me as Mestre the Padre Frey Francisco Negrão, who taught me to read and write. Under his instructions I learnt very good customs and etiquette and some special habits which Royal persons employ. Though I am a Chingala by blood I am a Portuguese in my ways and affections" (D. 12).

A more saddening confession it is not easy to imagine ; his pride of race and country were destroyed, and in place of the fervid patriotism which alone befitted a Prince of the Royal family in this, the long-drawn-out death agony of his people, there was substituted an ape-like imitation of Portuguese habits and ways of thought.

The Prince himself realised that this unfortunate upbringing had led to his being passed over in favour of his younger brother as the successor to the Throne. "It may well be" he bitterly commented "that this is the chief reason for my losing my kingdom, treasures, the Queen my wife, my son and all that I possessed." (D. 12).

"Your Excellency can well rely on my promises, though you see me in this condition. God and the world know that the affection which I always had for the Portuguese has brought me there," he wrote to the Viceroy (D. 12). "This Prince had always during the lifetime of his father shown himself friendly to the Portuguese," admitted that official (D. 4). "I have no confidence in my own people," the Prince could bring himself to write; whereas in regard to the Portuguese adventurer Simão de Oliveyra, "in him alone do I have reliance........I confide to him my life and my good name and other ambitions." (D. 1, 2).

As is so often the case with men of his race, his vanity was almost as great as it was childlike. He had his full share in the human weakness of loving to be patronised by the men in power. Resounding honorifics were to him as acceptable a compensation for the loss of the reality of power, as they are to-day among his countrymen.

The ceremony on the 8th of December, 1646, at the Church of São Francisco, a comedy and a tragedy combined, fittingly closed the education of the Prince. Heralded by his green pennant the Prince advanced down the steps leading from his house to where the Portuguese fidalgos stood bareheaded to receive and escort him to the Church. Little of the Sinhalese could be seen in him, for he was dressed in the latest Portuguese mode, from his velvet bonnet with its high aigrette down to his satin-lined shoes. The crowds pressed round him and shouted *viva* and threw flowers towards him, so that the stout halberdiers found it a difficult task to keep the passage clear. At the Church door the great Viceroy awaited him,—"this black" as his predecessor had styled him,—and led him by the hand within to where Patriarch and Primate witnessed his baptism. Thereupon his one remaining emblem of Sinhalese Royalty, his beautiful Eagle pendant, was removed from round his neck and offered to the Church, and in its stead the Viceroy placed on his head a crown of gold, with which the new Emperor went back home amidst much rejoicing.

Such was the recompense he obtained for the loss of race and country.

DOCUMENT 1.

Vijaya Pala to the Viceroy.

Your Lordship will know how the King of Uva, my brother, died and left me as heir to both his kingdom and his treasures, which were not few. My brother the King of Candia, as he is powerful, seized hold of everything and sent me certain chests of *larin* and some other articles which I was not willing to accept. Symão d'Oliveira was present; it is he whom I asked if he would take this letter to your Lordship, because in him alone do I have reliance: and everything else I discussed and arranged with him, for every confidence can be placed in so great a cavalheiro, as the Hollanders who had come to this kingdom proclaimed, which they did in his presence before me. I will greatly esteem it if your Lordship will give him a position when he comes, as it is time to bring him forward; and thus your Lordship will do me a favour by giving him an authority in His Majesty's name, fastened and sealed, that he may keep it in his possession so that I may be able with greater security to pass over to receive favours from His Majesty and from your Lordship. In this should be declared that no General or Captain should prevent my coming to your Lordship, from whom I expect to receive many favours.

Your Lordship will also know that the Kingdom of Candia belongs to me as the elder brother, and all this I lost in consequence of the great friendship which I have for the Portuguese, as is well known ; and I am hoping that what I lost through my affection for them will be restored by them. It will be a kindness if there is no delay regarding what I am asking here. Simão d'Oliveira will say the rest ; he is unwilling to receive any favours from me.

Our Lord keep your Lordship for many years.

Candia, the 10th of October, 1634.

King Vigiapaia.

(Documentos Remettidos da India, Archivo Nacional da Torre do Tombo, Lisboa ; Livro 35 f. 323).

DOCUMENT 2

Vijaya Pala to the Viceroy.

I learnt from a letter which I received from Simão d'Oliveira, written at Coilão on the 15th of April, 1635, that he was not crossing to India as a serious illness from which he suffered, prevented him. I also learnt that he was keeping in his possession the letter which I gave him for your Lordship, because I had instructed him not to entrust it to anyone.

Once more your Lordship may know that it was the Will of God that the King my father should die and he wished to recompense me for saving him from death many times, and for disinheriting me, by recommending me much to my brother. After all he whom I respected is dead. It is time your Lordship should do me a favour, as all you do will be for the good of the State : because I am not looking for anything else than to render the greatest service to His Majesty. I repeat to your Lordship, that for my matters to be successful, secrecy is what must be maintained therein. I have no confidence in my own people nor in the General, nor in the City of Columbo, for we know all their secrets. Here I think it pleased God that Simão d'Oliveira should come to this Matale ; as he was already so well known among my people, by his great efforts he relieved me of certain hesitations which I had about setting my designs on foot and from them I learnt his worth, and so I confide to him my life and my good name and other ambitions. Through the whole of April, 1636, I await a reply from your Lordship, whose life may our Lord increase for many years.

Candia, 2nd of October, 1635.

King Vijaya Pala.

(Doc. Rem. Livro, 35, f. 325).

DOCUMENT 3

Viceroy to the King.

At the present time the affairs of Candia are quiet as the old King is dead and his youngest son, whom he left installed in the kingdom, is ruling. Information has been received that the elder son, seeing himself treated with disfavour and kept out of possession of what appertains to him, intends to pass over to us. It is realised that should it happen thus it will be a great advantage, and I am ordering Diogo de Mello to seize every advance which this Prince makes, in order to get him within your Majesty's dominions. These latter are in need of food, wherefore I have sent instructions to Negapatão and other ports, that the largest possible quantity of surplus food may be despatched from them ; in March there will start from here everything possible with the other necessary supplies.

God protect the Catholic and Royal person of your Majesty, as Christendom and we your vassals have need.

From Goa, the 19th of February, 1636.

(Doc. Rem. Livro 33, f. 251 vo.)

DOCUMENT 4

Viceroy to the King.

After I had written to your Majesty the other letter regarding the affairs of Ceilão which is going by this *via*, there came to me letters from Vijaya Pala, Prince of Candia, the elder son of the deceased King, to whom belongs of right the kingdom which his younger brother usurped from him at the instigation of his father. In these he tells me of the disfavour with which the King his brother is treating him, and of the resolution which he has taken to pass over to us, asking me for an authority that the Captain-General of Ceilão or any other person should not prevent his coming to your Majesty's territory, and that I should send it through Simão d'Oliveira, who brought the said letters, because he confided this secret to him alone. As this is a matter of such great service to your Majesty, the Council to whom I referred the information, agreed that the said authority should be issued to him at once, and be forwarded without delay through the same Simão d'Oliveira, with instructions to communicate the matter by word of mouth to the General, so that in this way the secret would not be revealed : and to tell him to stand ready to receive the Prince and to help him as is found needful, for it is realised that this is the best method of reducing that Island under our authority, or at least of bringing matters there to a better state : for this Prince has always, during the lifetime of the King his father, shown himself friendly to the Portuguese, regarding which it seems to me right to give your Majesty an account by this letter, and to forward to you a copy of the letters of the said Prince and of the Resolution of the Council.

God protect, etc.

At Goa, the 28th of February, 1636.

(Doc. Rem. Livro 33, f. 252).

DOCUMENT 5

Queen Margidaly to the Viceroy.

With regard to the instructions which you sent for the reception and kind treatment of the Prince of

Matale, I approve on all points the orders you have given.

(Doc. Rem. Livro 40 ff 31-32 vo.).

DOCUMENT 6.

Viceroy to the King.

The intention which the Prince of Matale had of passing over to us, has led to no result in consequence of the natural fickleness of this race and the little confidence which as a rule can be placed in it.

Goa. 6th December, 1637.

(Doc. Rem. Liv. 40, ff 31-32 em margem)

DOCUMENT 7.

Diogo de Mello to Vijaya Pala.[20]

A letter from Your Highness has reached me which states that you have been informed of the arrival of Antonio Malchiado of Goa with goods and curiosities which he wished to take to Candia, asking me for permission to do so. Your Highness cannot be ignorant of what is taking place at Batticalo and that Raja Sinha your brother has made an alliance with the Dutch, the subjects of and rebels against the King of Portugal, pirates in the whole of India, hated of all Indian potentates as they were also formerly by your predecessors. Under the cloak of friendship they have equipped a fleet, but have been defeated near the aforementioned forts as they deserve. Raja Sinha has broken the alliance which the King his predecessor had made with us many years ago. We have strictly kept to it and are also willing to keep it with the present King, but we must treat friends as friends and enemies as enemies. We have on several occasions shown our willingness to give our assistance and lend our services as a condition of peace and amity required. We take God to witness to this assertion. Let the Dutch who are called to drive us out of the Island, freely come; but I predict for this kingdom ruin and trouble if they take our place. We are innocent of the consequences. The Emperor deserves all the blame. We beg Your Highness to consider the perils to which the harbours under Your Highness' jurisdiction will be exposed.

I have informed the Viceroy of Goa of the inconsiderate action of king Raja Sinha and that we are now at war. If you think it necessary to show him the letter, you are at liberty to do so. He would not read a letter of mine if I were to write to His Majesty.

In the town of Columbo, 21st Nov., 1637.

Diogo de Mello de Castro.

(Hague Archives: India Office Translations.)

DOCUMENT 8.

Viceroy to King.

......and it is not known if out of the whole of this force one man has escaped alive, except that some people say that Fernão de Mendoça, the same Diogo de

Mello's nephew, with three or four others were taken prisoner by the Prince of Matale, named Vijaya Pala, brother of the very King of Candia, Mahastana.

Goa, 29th August, 1638.
(Doc. Rem. Liv. 41, ff 7 vo.-9 vo.),

DOCUMENT 9.

The Captain-General of Ceylon to the Viceroy.

The King of Candia and his brother have fallen out and I do not think that there is likely to be a reconciliation between them; now it may be possible that they are willing to have relations with us.

12th Nov., 1640,
(Doc. Rem. Livro. 47, ff 86-87).

DOCUMENT 10.

Viceroy to the King.

These are all the works of God, because as the result of this rupture and from the fact that this Prince is very friendly towards the Portuguese, important results are expected.

Goa, 19th January, 1641,
(Doc. Rem. Livro 47, ff 85-85 vo.).

DOCUMENT 11.

Vijaya Pala to all Hollanders,

whether in our forts or in their ships, and to all their Governors of low and high degree.[21]

In the name of God,

I, Vijaya Pala Hareya (Kumaraya ?) am a lord of lords, a god of lords, great as the sea, shining as the

Sun, lord of three worlds, who speaks the truth, being of so great understanding that I fathom all things, and who takes under his protection those who seek his aid, this letter I write.

You are aware of all the harm my brother Raja Sinha has done me. I find no words in which to relate what he has made me suffer. It is his fault that I am a prisoner here, for he has closed against me the road from Gale to Batticaloa. I have been always ready for the service of my brother and often helped him in fighting the Portuguese, but he has repaid my good offices with evil doings.

Before I came here to this frightful hell I communicated all these things to the Captain of Batticaloa, hoping he would help me, but he did not even send me an answer.

I then went to Columbo and on the ninth day after my arrival some Dutch ships appeared off the roads. The Portuguese General was so frightened at this event that he begged me to protect the town with the soldiers under my command. The place was then committed to my sole charge, but to my great gr[illegible] the Dutch did not land nor did they give me a chance of communicating with them. The General thereupon begged of me to find some means to poison all the Dutch in Galle. I told him that when my brother had acted treacherously towards the Admiral of the Dutch. I had upbraided him for it, and they could not now expect that I should act the same part as I condemned in my brother. After that they did not trust me any longer. I was then asked to take the oath of allegiance to the King of Portugal, which I promised to do as soon as the King's letters should have arrived. They reproached me for having killed two Generals of the Portuguese and sent a number of elephants to the Dutch at Cottiara. They asked me what good the Dutch had ever done to us that I should show them such affection. They said that peace was now concluded between Portugal and the country of the Dutch and that Gale would soon be restored to the Portuguese. A few days later letters were shown to me in which it was stated that the General was made the lord of Gale until the third generation, and that the Prince of Orange and my brother the King of Ceylon would soon be prisoners in his hands. I was so furious at these statements that I struck the messenger. When this came to the ears of the Governor he sent a body of soldiers against me. At that time I had 2,000 men with me. We had already engaged in a fight and half a dozen Portuguese been killed, when the clergy and several of the residents came out of the town and proposed that we should make peace. Three Dutchmen who had joined my forces were hanged by the Portuguese. I managed to save a few of your people by sending them to Gale and Candia.

I am now practically a prisoner of the Portuguese and cannot stay here any longer. I will come to whatever place you appoint. If you send a vessel to fetch me, I shall take ship : if you direct me to go by land, I shall travel overland. You need not distrust me, because Wimala Dharma Suriya made Maha Naya on the Dutch at Batticaloa or because my brother Raja Sinha is a traitor. I seek your friendship because you are a people of good faith, generous nature, great intelligence, and high reputation, such as no other nation possesses. You know that I am the rightful King of Ceylon. When I was still a child I loved the Dutch already and wished a treaty of alliance to be made with that people ; and now although old and a prisoner I still have the former affection for you.

I have written to you without fear. Should the Portuguese hear of it my life would not be safe, but I trust in your friendship that you will send to deliver me. If a vessel is to be sent, let there be some sign at the top of the mast that I may know it is for me. I will reward you with anything in my power. My land is rich in elephants, gold, and precious stones. Quick-silver is found in every place. All the treasures of my land will be yours.

I once gave my word to a Portuguese and kept it. Why should I act differently towards you? Every day that I am kept waiting for your answer will seem a year to me.

This letter may be read by any Dutchman into whose hands it falls. You are at liberty to translate its contents into Dutch and send it to Jacatara to the Governor or friends. Notwithstanding the peace having been concluded, the Portuguese have instructions to get possession of Gale by artifice. If anything of importance happens I will inform you.

This is already the ninth letter I have written to you : I do not know how many have reached you. I am in a sad plight in this town of Colombo.

The Emperor Vigea Palla.

[This letter was received by the Dutch on 22nd Jan., 1643, and was then three months old.]

Hague Archives: India Office Translations.

DOCUMENT 12.

Vijaya Pala to the Viceroy.

Most Illustrious and Excellent Conde, Viceroy of India, I, Vijaya Pala, Emperador by the Grace of God, send much greeting to your Excellency, as one whom I greatly love and prize.

Senhor, I was waiting for the Hollanders to leave, so as to be able to visit Your Excellency. The Senhor Archbishop of Mira told me in your name what was for the salvation of my soul and the restoration of my honour and estate in the service of God and the King. The said Senhor Archbishop also told me as Your Excellency had said to him, and instructed me to write to you what I wished in reply.

I say, Senhor, that I am the son of the great King, whom God keeps; my mother was Dona Catherina, daughter of Jeavira Vedauntra,[22] grand-daughter of the Emperor Dom João. From her were born we three brothers, among whom was made a partition of the Kingdom of Candia. To Cumara Sinha, the eldest brother, was allotted the Kingdom of Uva; Candia to Ra Sinha; and that of Matale to me; while all three of us lived in the city of Candia, and the said brother was crowned as Emperador of all the Kingdoms, and we as his vassals (*sugeitos*). On the death of the said brother they in the same manner crowned me in the presence of my father. On his death ten or twelve years ago, Ra Sinha tyrannically usurped the Kingdoms, because my kindness of heart would not consent to the vassals killing him. So I remained in the Kingdom of Matale after the rupture with him, and always in hopes of recovering the rest with the help of the Portuguese, by whom for many years I was urged to come to Colombo.

To bring this about the Conde de Linhares sent me two safe conducts and presents, with great promises in the King's name that with Portuguese arms and the power of the nations he would place me in possession of the country. The Viceroy Pero da Silva Molle also sent me two, with presents, by Fernão de Mendonca; the Governor Antonio Telles de Menezes acted in the same way. Constantino Dessa four with many presents and a promise of the Seven Corlas, all in the Viceroy's name. Dom Jorge d' Almada two, with presents, always begging me to come. Diogo de Mello de Castro three; Dom Philip Mascarenhas one. When I was in Uva he sent me by a Lascarin of my ambassador a letter which Ra Sinha wrote to the said General, which contained promises, so that he should not give me the help which he had at his disposal in case of need. The same Dom Philip Mascarenhas wrote to Sofragão that I should come immediately to help the city of the King my brother; so long as he did not occupy Candia, he would give me the Seven Corlas. In conformity with this I left everything and came to Columbo, relying on his word, along with 2,000 fighting men, 400 with *espingardas*, 250 with *pedreneiras*, two companies of Canarese with *arcabuzes*, 94 foot muskets, 50 Kaffirs, 10 *trilhains*,[23] 200 attendants who carried munitions and for other work, 10 Portuguese, Mudaliars, Dissavas, 3 Bandaras, and a Prince who is my Captain Major of the Field; with these and my Royal insignia and royal music.[24] I came giving courage confidence and zeal to all at a time that it was under siege by sea and land, and where died 191. Better at Seitavaca, in the arrayals and in all the other occasions which arose.

I came relying on a letter of a General apart from numerous promises; and he paid me finally with this. Seeing the injustice I came to Your Excellency's presence. I received and am receiving from your hands many honours and favours, and such entertainment that I could have lost my health by excess. In a word, I shall learn to acknowledge all this as what I am, if God give me the opportunity.

I am also relating to Your Excellency, since you stand to-day in place of the King, how I spent money. I pledged my jewels to maintain my men who till now are engaged in the service of the said Senhor, because money for expenses ran short; and as in my opinion Dom Philip Mascarenhas was not sufficient, I helped with my men at times; even the Senhor Bishop of Cochin was necessary for me to ask for a loan from outside, as is well known.

I state, Senhor, that I was born with a strong predilection for the Portuguese nation. In my earliest years, greatly to the satisfaction of the Queen my mother, there was assigned to me as Mestre the Padre Frey Francisco Negrão, who taught me to read and write. Under his instruction I learnt very good customs and etiquette and some special habits which Royal persons employ. Though I am a Chingala by blood, I am a Portuguese in my ways and my affections; it may well be that this is the chief reason for my losing my Kingdom, treasures, the Queen my wife, my son[25] and all that I possessed, at last reaching this state in which I see myself.

I shall not bring to Your Excellency's recollection some very small acts of kindness which I always did to the Portuguese, for to write them would need several folios of paper ; I only mention what all who come from Ceilão will tell Your Excellency ; how I was the refuge of everyone in the many disasters they suffered, both of Constantino Dessa as of Diogo de Mello de Castro ; and at last I came to be the prisoner of Ra Sinha the tyrant, full of wounds through defending the Portuguese, whose images of God and your Lady and the Saints I ever treated with all veneration, though much against the wish of the said tyrant. Afterwards I handed them to the Senhor Bishop of Cochim, Dom Frei Miguel Rangel, and his Vicar-General, the Padre Frei Francisco da Fonsequa ; and then in Colombo they took from me at the sack of my house, an infant Jesus. Dom Alvaro took from me on the way a Reliquary ; up to now he has not returned it to me. So that I was always half a Christian ; and now with the favours Your Excellency has done me, and the arguments of the Senhor Archbishop of Mira who to-day is showing me the road I have to follow, I am determined to become a Christian. The conditions which I demand are not due to any lack of desire to become one ; but because I am what I am and have a wife and son, it is my duty to establish my matters and to arrange them for the service of God our Lord and the salvation of myself and my vassals.

Therefore I demand that Your Excellency should restore to me everything which Dom Philipe Mascarenhas took from me—gold, precious stones, arms and royal insignia, not troubling about other articles.

Secondly, that I should be treated as the Emperador's grandson, allowing me an expenditure in accordance with my dignity.

Thirdly, that the Seven Corlas should be given to me, as promised by Constantino Dessa, Dom Antonio Mascarenhas, and Dom Philipe Mascarenhas, in the King's name, so long as they do not take possession of Candia.

Fourthly, a General who shall be my friend, a God-fearing man who will respect me as his superior, to look after the war and to help me to win back my kingdom.

Finally, in the first Moncão, send me back to Ceilão, as that concerns my honour ; for those who saw me insulted and robbed there complaining as a private fidalgo, should now see me honoured and favoured under my proper title by a Viceroy of India who is in place of the King himself.

If you do this which I state, in addition to becoming a Christian, I promise to swear to an offensive and defensive league with the King, and everything else which is not against my honour and what concerns my dignity. Your Excellency can well rely on my promises, though you see me in this condition. God and the world knows that the affection which I always had for the Portuguese has brought me there. And now it will be with a double sense of obligation, for the affection which Your Excellency has shown me ; and so you should fix your eyes on what I am and what I have done, even pouring out my blood for them.

As to what I demand and promise, do me the favour of ordering this statement to be examined in the Council of State ; and there should be summoned to it some persons who know thereof and are acquainted with me, such as the Bishop of Cochim, his Vicar-General, the Padre Frey João de Tarrin, Francisco de Britto, Fernão de Mendonca ; and if there is anything written by Dom Philipe Mascarenhas against me, I stand quite prepared to give full satisfaction and such explanation as will be sufficient for Your Excellency, taking for my witnesses God our Lord and the persons of the Cidade ; for I do not believe that the King Dom João and his Holiness, of whom I am a son by affection, will fail to acknowledge these my reasonable demands, along with such promises : nor will they wish that I should be worried with acts of oppression. Much less ought I to expect that from your Excellency, in whom I have found such great marks of friendship and affection.

God preserve the person of Your Excellency.

Written at the Convent of São Francisco on the first of May, 1643.

You can forgive the sorry style of this letter because it is prepared by me who do not yet know to write or draw up memorials.

Emperador Vigiapala.

(Doc. Rem. Livro. 54, ff. 9-12).

DOCUMENT 13.

Pope Urbano viii. to Vijaya Pala.

Son, Vija, we wish you health and prosperity. In humility let us render many immortal thanks to the most high Lord, the author of all good things. As soon as we saw and read your Majesty's letter with the evidence of the Archbishop of Mira, that your Majesty, fired by love of the Christian religion, was being instructed in the path of your salvation as a Senhor most wise and most learned in tongues and sciences, and desired as speedily as possible to receive the water of Holy baptism : though we were engaged with many cares and anxieties, yet this welcome news in the highest degree cheered and refreshed us ; for this is the ship of São Pedro, outside which there is no salvation, and all are lost. We govern by the Grace of God, which never can fail. For your Majesty knows that there is no matter which the solicitude of the Pope strives after with greater desire than that all the races, although far removed from us and set amidst the deceits and wiles of the devil, should be wrested from him, and placed in the ship of São Pedro, where they may with ease cast anchor in the harbour of salvation.

God our Lord confirm the work which he has begun in your Majesty, and may this intent so holy reach a happy end ; it will be possible to expect with the utmost certainty the help of the divine clemency which cannot fail. And when your Majesty sees yourself among the dangers and vexations of your enemies and malignant and jealous men, then you will find that there cannot be wanting a very strong castle of David, where your crowned royal virtue can serve Jesus Christ in freedom, bringing the vassals of the Kings in your Majesty's Estates to the knowledge of the same Lord, by your royal arm, effectively, as we hope. In which we must always take pleasure and give our blessing to your undertakings.

We shall not permit that our very great Apostolic favours and the paternal love which we have towards your Majesty should be in vain, nor should anything which would be helpful or increase the Royal Estate of your Majesty, be neglected.

In the meantime we are awaiting with great desire that day of Jubilee and gladness in which news must come to us that we can be certain that your Majesty has enlisted under the banner of Jesus Christ along with the rest of the Christian Kings and Princes, to receive you in our arms with great joy and due welcome, when your Majesty as I expect sends me ambassadors who in your royal name may promise loyal obedience to the Apostolic See.

May He in whose hands lie the hearts of Kings and Lords govern your Majesty's royal acts and deeds ; to that Lord we earnestly pray to increase and place on the pinnacle of all happiness the person and royal Estate of your Majesty.

Done in Rome at São Pedro under the Seal of the Fisherman, the 19th of March, 1644.

Urbano VIII Julius.

(Doc. Rem. Livro 61, f 210).

DOCUMENT 14.

King to Viceroy.

Conde, Viceroy of India, friend,

I, the King, send you much greeting as to one whom I love. Along with this letter there is forwarded to you the copy of another which the Emperador Vigia Pala wrote to me, in which he gives me an account of certain incidents which you will learn therefrom. And because it is my desire that he should realise the good will which I have to assist him in his difficulties and in the acts of injustice which he says are inflicted on him by some Ministers of mine, and it is right that favour and kindness should be shown to him in everything which concerns him, I direct and charge you to advise me of the nature of his requests and to cause them to be examined and discussed in the Council of State, and to send me your opinion with all clearness and precision, with everything else which presents itself to you regarding this man; for it is my wish to know them with certainty and exactitude. In the meanwhile, you should order that all good entertainment for which there is occasion be rendered to him.

Written at Lisboa, the 4th of April, 1644.

The King.

(Doc. Rem. Livro 48, f. 301).

DOCUMENT 15.

Viceroy to King.

It will be three years next March that the Prince of Matale came to this city, and the evil acts and wicked proceedings which this black committed when he was in Columbo under your Majesty's protection were well known to the General Dom Philippe Mascarenhas; for he came to look for refuge from his brother the King of Candia, who wished to kill him. The General sent him to Goa in six ships of the Armada with all the dignity and respect which was due to the name of Prince, which he does not deserve, and I am satisfied that during the time he was in Columbo he was treated by the said General Dom Philippe Mascarenhas in the same fashion, for he gave him not only what was necessary for his maintenance, but everything else he demanded, in order to keep him contented and satisfied, as he knew that such would be to your Highness' service.

But as this Prince is so changeable and restless, ignoring the truth of what I have said, he is unjustly complaining to your Majesty both against the same General and also against Dom Alvaro de Ataide who came as Captain Major of that Armada in which he arrived here; from the day of his landing up till now there is being given to him from your Majesty's Royal Fazenda 329 xerafims a month for the expenses of his person, paid with great punctuality; perhaps what he wrote to Your Majesty about the General of Ceilão he will do to-morrow about the Conde de Aveiras. I think your Majesty should be pleased to send no reply to his letters, for he does not deserve it owing to his behaviour. As I have reported, this is notorious throughout the whole of India, so that I consider it unnecessary to dwell on it with greater detail.

God protect, etc.

Goa, the— of January, 1645.

(Doc. Rem. Livro 48, f. 301).

DOCUMENT 16.

King to Viceroy.

Viceroy of India,

I, the King, send you much greeting as to one whom I love.

The Prince of Candia, son of the King of Candia, complained to me that they robbed him in Ceilão and ill-treated him after he had retired to the city of Columbo on the directions of the Captain-General of that Island. I strictly enjoin you to order an inquiry into that matter, and if you find that the said robbery was committed on him, satisfaction for it must be given him by the persons who were concerned therein and they must be punished as the justice of the case demands; and because I am advised that his *espingarda* was taken away from the said Prince as he was standing already in his house, you should make investigation to find out the truth about the incident and to punish the guilty.

You shall keep him under supervision so that he does not go to Ceilão, because of the prejudice which his person and residence will create there; nor, in order to avoid expense, should he come to this Reino: and as he reports that he desires to be baptised and become a Christian, requesting me to take him as my godson, I direct you that if he is arranging to accomplish this undertaking, you should be his god-father in my name, instructing you that he should be well treated, because he is not so: I expect from you that you will thus carry out this matter.

Written at Lisboa on the 13th of March, 1645.

I, the Secretary, Affonso de Barras Caminna, caused this to be written.

The King.

(Doc. Rem. Livro 56, f. 101).

DOCUMENT 17.

Viceroy to King.

Senhor,

This Prince of Candia retired to Columbo under my safe conduct when I was General of that Island, being compelled by the war which his brother was waging against him; and having thus found shelter at the expense of your Majesty's Fazenda with all the good treatment which I was able to give him, he began to open a secret correspondence with the Hollanders with the intention of passing over to them: such is his fickleness. His letters and those of the Hollanders themselves regarding this matter, came into my hands. I received the same information through João de Sousa Pereira who at the time held the Captaincy of Sam Thome, and obtained it by way of the Hollanders of Palacate. As the matter was already far advanced and greater restlessness in that Island would arise from his joining them, I decided to secure his person and did so personally and took him to the Convent of São Françisco, from where I shipped him to India.

When I held this inquiry I ordered an inventory to be made in his presence of everything which he had and which he himself showed. Of this the original was given to him. As I have said, I shipped him with everything to India, to deliver him to the Conde de Aveyras, as was done. Having acted thus, only I could have caused him the loss and cheating of which he complains. Accordingly it will be convenient for your Majesty to order an inquiry on this subject through another, and because he also (charges) me with being present when, as he says, the espingarda was taken from him, about that your Majesty should consider it very certain that same plot would have been carried out by this Prince.

Regarding him the Conde de Aveyras now informs me that he has directed him to withdraw to a mud fort, as he was attempting to carry out from Goa the same as from Ceilão, though he was treated so well and at such expense to your Majesty's Fazenda.

I shall take care that he does not pass over to the Reino, for it always seems to me that it is not desirable that any other of his position should do this.

God protect, etc.

Cochim, the 31st of November, 1645.

(Doc. Rem. Livro 56, f. 211 *vo.*)

DOCUMENT 18

A True Account of the Baptism of Theodosio,

Emperor of Ceilão, King of Candia, Uva and Matale, Vassal of the King Our Lord, Dom João IV.

When troubles are permitted by the Providence of God, they always result in his greater glory, and benefit to the sufferer's soul of higher worth than all the world's kingdoms and empires; where illustrations were lacking, sufficient is that of this Prince who, while in the darkness of heathendom, saw himself tyranically deprived of his Estate, whence arose for him the blessing of gaining the Catholic Faith, as we shall see.

The Emperor of Ceilão Vigiapala, King of Candia, Uva and Matale, lawful heir of and successor to that splendid Estate, is a Prince of great parts both natural and acquired; for besides being graceful there can be seen in his stature and bearing the Majesty worthy of an Empire, which Fortune, ever jealous of the highest worth, has opposed. He is gifted with high courage and spirit as will appear from the enterprises in which he has figured, always to help the Portuguese, along with whom he has fought in those regions in the service of this Crown, of which he is a Vassal, and maintained with us throughout a loyal friendship which was never interrupted. He is a great Cavalheiro, very skilled in all arts which become a Prince. He speaks Portuguese with much fluency and ease; in consequence of his following our arms he was defeated in the field and took refuge in the Cidade of Columbo from whence he came to Goa, the head and Metropolis of the Estado of India.

The Archbishop of Mira, Dom Frey Francisco Antonio, was very anxious to win him to our Holy Catholic Faith, and so laboured earnestly for his conversion, both to exalt the Law of Christ, which was his chief object, as also to convey to the High Pontiff, Vicar of Christ on Earth, that His Majesty the King our Lord has for Vassals an Emperor and Christian Kings, whereby he may appraise the favours of which a son so obedient to him, is deserving from the Apostolic See: and that in climes so remote he is making known the Standard of Faith and Christian religion, and thus it may be published among Christian Kings and Princes.

He found in the disposition of this Prince a great inclination towards his intent, and so it was very easy to persuade him to declare that he desired to receive the Law of Christ our Lord and to be baptised with other Princes, fidalgos, and members of his Casa: towards which also he derived some special encouragement and inducement from the compliment of a Brief from the High Pontiff Urbano VIII., issued at Rome on the 19th of March, 1644, addressed to himself and obtained by means of the self-same Archbishop of Mira.

At length the time came at which the Emperor resolved to carry his wishes into effect and receive the Holy Baptism, for which he selected the Church and Monastery of Sam Francisco, which was decorated with the beauty and elaboration suited to an Act so important. The day was a Saturday, the eighth of December, 1646, on which day the Church observes the Feast of the Immaculate Conception of Our Lady the Virgin, to whom this Prince was greatly devoted even while he was a heathen. It was arranged that the Most Illustrious Senhor, the Archbishop of Mira, should baptize him, and that the rest of the Prelados should be present; and in a word that the act should be celebrated with the utmost pomp and display possible. Although definite notice of this did not reach many, the great concourse of people who assembled with much rejoicing, was remarkable.

The Emperor came out of his Casa, there being borne before him a green banner (guião) displaying an Imperial Eagle embroidered in gold and encrusted with many and very costly precious stones on the one side, and on the other the Quinas of our Portuguese arms—the precious device of our Redemption—all of gems of exceeding great value. He was dressed in high black shoes lined with white satin, white stockings, and a short cloak lined with white, with rich buttons of gold, a round bonnet of black velvet, with buckles (?) of the finest diamonds, and at the base of the aigrette a jewel of great value encircled by a large number of the costliest pearls, with a white waistcoat, slashed and covered with gold lace over a vest of white tissue. Round his neck he wore an Eagle set in a scallop shell, adorned and made entirely of rubies.[26] Twenty attendants dressed in taffety of colours accompanied him.

As he went down the steps with this escort, by the Viceroy's orders all the fidalgos clothed in their holiday dress stood awaiting him, and after all had made him a deep reverence, they accompanied him walking in front bareheaded, and he came behind covered. That was the order which had been given. A guard of halberdiers walked on the one side and the other, to keep back the dense crowd which came to see an Act so festive and a setting so majestic. Behind the Prince came Diogo Dias de Coimbra, Cavalheiro of the Order of Christ, who came on special orders owing to his peculiar authority and experience, to instruct him as to the procedure of the Curia in ceremonial matters, and to make the oration on his behalf; and by him went a Prince of his kingdom with the Crown and Sceptre covered with cloth of tissue.

In this fashion and amidst many *vivas* from the children, tears from the old folk, rejoicings and blessings from all, they reached the gate of the Church where the Viceroy Dom Felipe Mascarenhas had already arrived and stood waiting for him, along with the Archbishop Primate Dom Frey Francisco dos Martyres, and the Patriarch of Ethiopia. As soon as they met they exchanged greetings and the Viceroy took him by the hand, and so they advanced in the same order as far as the first altar where the Archbishop of Mira was standing, robed in his pontificals, and addressed to him the preliminary questions. This being concluded and after making his reverence, they advanced to the middle of the Church where was a second altar most richly adorned with hangings. Here the Emperor recited the Credo and other customary prayers, and after making his obeisances and due respects, they proceeded as far as the Cross, where was a third altar, at which they were to baptise him, and the celebration of this Act began. On reaching therein the words " I renounce Sathan," Diogo Dias de Coimbra removed from the Emperor's neck the Imperial Eagle which he wore, and turning to the Most Illustrious Senhor, the Archbishop Primate, he handed it to him with these few words :—

" His Majesty the Emperor Vigiapala, King of Candia, Uva and Matale, in token that with all his heart he eschews, abominates and renounces all the errors of heathendom and the vanities of the world, delivers to you, Most Illustrious Senhor, this Imperial Eagle, as an emblem heathen and profane, desiring that you may consecrate it with the sign of the sacred Cross of Christ our Lord, whose holy Faith he solemnly promises to observe, and to make all his vassals observe, until his death."

This brief address being concluded they went on with the ceremonies which the Church employs in administering the Sacrament of Baptism, with all the magnificence which was demanded by the position of the parties baptised and baptising, and of the God-fathers, who were the Viceroy Dom Felipe Mascarenhas, the Senhor Archbishop Primate, and the Patriarch of Ethiopia; and there was given to him the name of Theodosio, out of respect to the Prince Dom Theodosio, our Senhor the Prince, heir of the Lusitanian monarchy, without over-looking that it was a great augury of good fortune that the Divine Majesty should permit to be given to this Emperor and that there should be placed on him the name of a Christian Emperor, Spanish, ever unconquered, and so favoured of heaven that he and the minds in alliance with him, fought in his favour against his enemies, as truthfully sang the great poet Claudianus.

After the God-fathers had laid their hands on the head of the baptised, Diogo Dias de Coimbra turned to the Archbishop of Mira, who baptised, and addressed these words to him:—"His Majesty the Emperor Theodosio, as your Most Illustrious Lordship stands as baptiser in the place of Christ our Lord, and as you have performed this act on the orders of the Supreme Pontiff, in token of the obedience which he renders to the same Supreme Pontiff Innocencio the Tenth, our Senhor and father, and to his lawful successors, humbles himself first before your Most Illustrious Lordship, and next before the Most Illustrious Senhor Primate, who by virtue of his office stands in place of His Holiness as Pastor of the whole of the Estado of India."

The Emperor immediately made his reverence at the feet of the baptising Archbishop, who checked him and would not consent to his going on his knees, and embraced him, the Patriarch, Primate and Viceroy doing the same. Forthwith the same Diogo Dias de Coimbra, taking the Emperor's Sceptre and Crown from the hand of the Prince, who as we have stated was bearing them, removed the cloth of tissue with which they came covered, and holding them in his hand and making a reverence to the Viceroy Dom Felipe Mascarenhas in the name of the King our Lord, whom by virtue of his office he represented, made before him in the name of the baptised Emperor the act and acknowledgment of fealty and vassalage in the form following :—

" Senhor,

The Emperor Theodosio, as your Excellency stands in place of the Most High and Powerful King and our Senhor Dom João IV., his brother, offers to your Excellency this Crown and Sceptre, as security for the promise which he gives to maintain his fealty to His Majesty, whom God preserve : hoping from your greatness for much favour and help, so as thereby to obtain many victories against the rebels, enemies of the Holy Catholic Faith; and all the success and victories which he obtains will be only for the glory of God our Lord. and the spread of Christianity and in order that thereby may be increased the Realms and the Renown of the Most High and Powerful King and our Lord, Dom João IV., his brother."

As soon as Diogo Dias de Coimbra closed this speech and act, the Viceroy took the Crown in his hand and placed it on the head of the Emperor, who when this was done, turned and embraced the Viceroy; the same Diogo Dias removed the Crown from his head, and the Emperor turned and made his reverences to the Archbishops and the Patriarch, and the Viceroy placed the Crown a second time on him; whereupon he gracefully and with majesty taking three steps forward, made a profound reverence to the altar; and the same Diogo Dias removed the Crown from him, and the Te Deum Laudamus was begun with the music of very melodious voices. Then taking him by the hand and placing him in the middle, the Viceroy on his right hand and the Prelates all together and all covered, they went and sat down in a room of the Convent, in which there was throughout given to him the best place with a rich sofa which was fitted there. After staying here in this same fashion for a short time, he led him as far as the Porter's Lodge, from where after an exchange of courtesies, he went in the midst of his guard with all the fidalgos uncovered, and he covered, in the same order in which he first came, as far as his own Casa, which was in front of the same Convent.

While they were escorting him thus on his leaving the Church, the Emperor's *criados* were being baptised and they along with those who were already baptised; made a total of ninety and four, including among them four Princes of that Empire of Ceilão, Dom João da Sylva, General of the Army, Dom Thome da Sylva, Dom João da Menezes, and the Ambassador Dom Fernando de Castro, two Captains Mor, and two Captains of Infantry. The people who were present at these acts and ceremonies were so numerous, that although the Church is very capacious and large it was not possible to accommodate them within; and so as the choir, galleries, doors and pillars were not sufficient, they could not even be contained within the Church yard; for the crowd was very great, all with loud *vivas* and acclamations scattering thick showers of garlands and flowers: emblems of the hopes of the great good fortune which God will be pleased to give for the increase of his glory, the restoration of this Prince, victories and the spread of the majesty and grandeur of the Most High and Powerful King and our Lord Dom João IV., whom God preserve.

Certificate of the Archbishop of Mira.

On the 8th of December, 1646, I baptised Dom Theodosio, Emperor of Candia, Uva and Matale, in the presence of Dom Felipe Mascarenhas, Viceroy of India, and of the Archbishop Primate and the Patriarch of Ethiopia. The said baptism took place in the manner contained in this document, in the presence of all the fidalgos and nobles of India, and in narrating this truthfully I certify to it with my right hand placed on my breast and I have executed this present as I was requested.

In Goa, the 10th of February, 1647.

Frey Franciscus Antonius,
Archbishop of Mira.

In Lisboa, with the necessary Licenses.
By Manoel Gomez de Carvalho in the year 1648.

DOCUMENT 19

Dom Duarte de Bragança to the King.

When the Emperador my Senhor was in the Kingdom of Uva with all prosperity and strength, fighting with the Prince his younger brother and a tyrant, the chief enemy of himself and of the Portuguese nation, Dom Felipe Mascarenhas who was Captain-General of Ceilão, seeing himself hard pressed by enemies, sent a letter by Manoel da Silveira de Villalobos, the ambassador, in the name of the King Dom João, and a present of a lion of gold, the ambassador of Holland being at the Court of the Emperador my Senhor. In this he asked him to be pleased to assist him in his peril, seeing that he always helped and protected the Portuguese in similar straits and in all the disasters they had suffered in the Empire of Candia ; he pledged his word in the name of the King Dom João to help with men and other necessaries to win back the Empire which the Emperador my Senhor lost through his friendship for this nation, (just as had already promised the Viceroys the Conde de Linhares, Pedro da Silva, Antonio Telles de Menezes, and the Conde de Aveyras, as also the Generals Constantino de Sa, Dom Jorge de Almeida, Diogo de Mello de Castro, and Dom Antonio Mascarenhas, all by writings which the Emperador my Senhor now keeps in safe custody, and which at some time he will send and show to some Minister or Governor).

In the meantime he would entertain him with all courtesy and due respect, providing the surplus expenses, and giving villages and Corlas which the Emperador my Senhor had sent to ask for through a Modeliar, to bring there his treasures and royal household and the families of his vassals of various grades who had to accompany him, and the royal state which his person and crown demanded, assuring him against injury and prejudice to his person and to his vassals while he remained in the territory of the King Dom João

Therefore, relying on the embassy, the Emperador my Senhor hastened with many thousands of fighting men, Captains, Dissavas, Mudaliars, and three Bandaras, his vassals, who are Condes and Marquises, with many Canarese and Kaffirs and Portuguese, former prisoners whom he took from the hands of enemies in various battles, and money and stores; among them was a nephew of the Prince de Telheiras,[27] his vassal, whom here two Portuguese servants of the Emperador my Senhor killed, for spreading stories against the person of their Senhor in revenge for the offence of the late Viceroy, who is his god-father.

With this state and force the Emperador came to Sofragão with the King's ambassador, repulsing the Hollanders, and there he released the arrayal of Antonio de Motta from an ambush laid by the tyrant Prince, although I did not wish to mention this true fact for a certain reason which I do not go into minutely so as not to prolong the story.

At this juncture the Governor wrote a letter very affectionately repeating his application and urging the Emperador, through Francisco Barbosa de Andrade, Captain Major that was, with one from the City, that he might be pleased to come with the utmost speed to the unprotected city, as it was besieged by powerful enemies by sea and land without soldiers to defend it, and numerous promises of various mattters which I do not specify, which may be seen in the said letters. In entire reliance the Emperador my Senhor came to Colombo with the said succour giving encouragement to all, bringing back many people from the lands below who were in revolt, and hidden in the woods for certain reasons. Here he helped them, dividing a part of his army among the four *arraiaes* of the King, supplying them with Canarins and Kaffirs, his prisoners, to carry munitions and stores, who till now are taking part in that *Conquista*.

In this fashion he helped and assisted them while he could, taking the defence of the fort of Nigumbo to his charge while he was in Ceilão, spending many lives and treasure in the restoration of the lands and the defence of the City. He subdued the Four Corlas which were in revolt, sending the said nephew of the Prince, his vassal, as General, with the rest of his army which remained, as is proved by the certificates which he holds from the Bishop of Cochim, the Guardião of São Francisco, the Vicar-General of the Holy Office, the Clerk of the Camara, and the Prior of Santo Augustinho, whom a brother of the said General killed there, and from other citizens. He also caused to be completed a portion of the moat of Mapane, all at the cost of his royal household.

After the war was ended and the treaty with the Hollanders proclaimed, some Ministers in return for all this schemed and laid a plot and robbed him of 900,000 cruzados in jewels alone, besides all the royal service of gold and silver, writing to him a letter in the name of the Hollanders. There was no need to feed him up with such tricks as he had shown his royal zeal and loyalty to the Portuguese nation on many occasions. When he came to India to demand justice before the Conde de Aveiras here, they robbed him further of more than 300,000 xerafims in various articles of jewellery, urging against him deceits

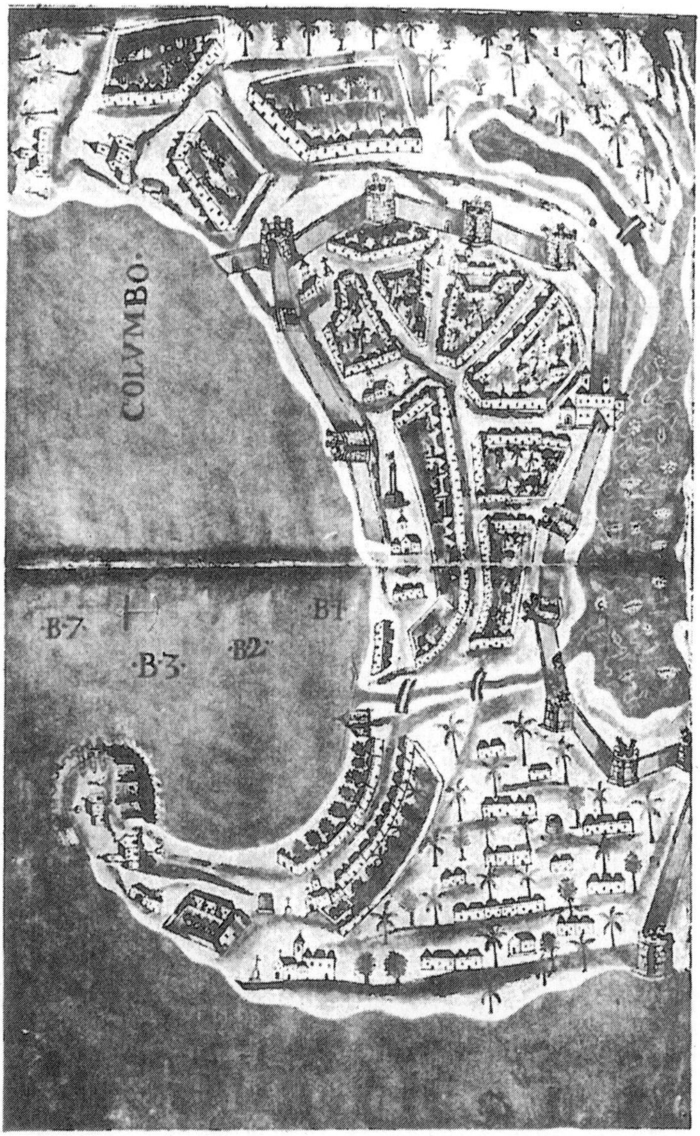

COLUMBO IN 1635

(SLOANE MSS. 197. BRITISH MUSEUM.)

and falsehoods so vivid ; notwithstanding this a Minister of the Court of the Viceroy who is now governing, committed further excesses, entering the house of the Emperor my master, robbing him and breaking the doors and locks of the royal chambers which were secured, and the keys in charge of the Ouvidor General Miguel Cirne, while he was at Murmagao, with the result that there were cast on the street, horses, men, boxes, coffers, and drawers, the bulk of them open, without any regard to the great offence and violence the said Meirinho committed.

Here he lost 50,000 xerafims in jewels of precious stones, and articles of adornment in gold, silver, velvet and brocade : about this too the Emperador my Senhor sent and protested before the Princes of the Church, the late Inquisitor, the prelates and ministers, giving them in private proof and details of the said jewels. Had not the Archbishop Primate, the Inquisitor, fidalgos and prelates of convents, kindly helped and assisted the Emperador with loans on his royal word, he could not support with bread this household of various grades, to wit, two Bandaras, three Mudaliars, fifteen fidalgos, besides pages, Portuguese officials and guards and other heathen, with the horses and numerous *Esmolas* and *merces* which he gave to widows, maidens, orphans and poor and crippled *soldados*, who continually came to him. And it is manifest to all that he has only one glory and grandeur, which is to be most kind and friendly to each and all except some as to whom he has reason for not being so. Even the Chaplain who says Mass in his royal chapel the Archbishop supports out of his poverty: not even for that has the Emperor my master now the means, because he is indebted to various parties in 33,000 xerafims on the security of the jewels which he pledged for the King's celebrations at the request of the Viceroys, and for the upkeep of his household. The allowance which the Viceroy assigned to him when he was not yet a Christian is not sufficient, not even for a week; such as it is, there is due to him 15,000 xerafims out of the said allowance, which has accumulated during the past years.

The Emperor my master requests the King Dom João, his brother and god-father, to send him to Ceilão to remain with the Captain-General till orders come regarding the other questions; if this is found a matter of difficulty, to send precise instructions to the Viceroy to treat him generally in accordance with his position and crown, and the King's greatness. The Princes of the Church and other fidalgos and Prelates of the Court treat him with so much courtesy, affection and respect: which is more to be imputed to the greatness of the King Dom João, whereupon the Viceroys have much cause to pay the Emperor my master in similar coin. Note the occasional visits out of respect for the place he fills—for a heathen ruler who came from Sunda in the time of the Governor Antonio Telles de Menezes was visited by him. No less did those of Ormuz do to that Prince: and what the Governors of Ceilão, who bear the name of King, did to the Senhor Emperador Dom João Prea Pandar[28] grandfather of the Emperador my master, on orders of the Kings of Portugal, the which is well known. Two attendants with the Habit of Christ waited on him: he as Emperador and brother of the King, gave them to whom he pleased. But he did not maintain such great ceremonious and majestic state as my master does to-day; and he obtained the Briefs of the Supreme Pontiff, so honourable and glorious to the Emperador my Senhor. Yet this was under an administration which usurped and took away another's cloak,[29] while to-day the King Dom João is the true and most just King of Portugal, who contrariwise gives increase to all. He will support and give order to support and maintain the Emperador my master against any monarch who desires to oppose him.

For this reason he did not go out up till now to any public ceremony or to visit the Churches, as he waits to do so under the express order and direction of the King with more distinction than any Senhor of India and Ceilão Taprobana, with the humility and sincere hope of a godson.

Therefore send directions how he should be treated at this Court and in the Churches. If this is not to be, he hopes for an order for him to pass to that Reino with his vassals and Royal State, so that when he is closer the King may recognize and see his affection and his deeds. He bears everything with great patience, tolerance and brightness, in the lively hope that the King his brother and godfather, is going to help and honour him in everything in a manner conforming to his greatness, though until now he has not done so in consequence of his pre-occupations.

God our Lord protect the Person, Estate and Majesty of the King Dom João IV. for many years.

Goa, on the 20th of January, 1649.

Prince, Grand Chamberlain of the Emperador of Candia, Dom Duarte de Bragança.

(Doc. Rem. Liv. 61, ff 209-211).

DOCUMENT 20

King to Viceroy.

Dom Philipe Mascarenhas, Viceroy, friend,

I, the King, send you much greeting.

The Emperador of Candia wrote to me giving me an account of the solemnity with which his baptism and coronation were celebrated, the number of attendants with which he was furnished, of whom some went on board ship when you ordered them, and about other details ; he begs me to send instructions to provide him with what is needed for the maintenance of himself and his household. And because I am considering the subject and also it is not possible to arrive at a decision thereon without your opinion and information, especially because in last year's *Vias* you did not write to me anything about the Emperador, until I send you other orders I strictly enjoin you to keep watch over his designs and actions, and that you should not under any circumstances agree to his absenting himself from that city or going to Ceilão or this Reino, and you must show him favour in every matter that is just and due and you should let him understand that I am so ordering, and report to me what action you take and what occurs to you.

Written at Lisbon on the 22nd of March, 1649.

The King.

(Doc. Rem. Livro 60, f 224).

DOCUMENT 21

Viceroy to the King.

* * *

Senhor,

It is also established that the document which was submitted to your Majesty by the King of Candia is entitled to little consideration, because when the Inquisitor João de Barras, on your Majesty's orders, held an inquiry about the robberies which he says were committed on him, it was ascertained that there was none found who would belong to the robbers. This King is very fantastic with little solidity in his affairs. Regarding his allowance a report has been made to your Majesty by another letter of this *Via*.

(Doc. Rem. Livro 61 f. 196).

DOCUMENT 22

King to Viceroy.

Count, Viceroy, friend,

I, the King, send you much greeting as to one whom I love.

In the *via* of my letters which you took in your company was one dated the 13th of April of last year, in which was written to me by the Patriarch of Ethiopia that the Emperador of Candia who is living in that city of Goa, suffered much want as he had a large number of people with him including four *grandes* from Ceilão, and because the 200 xerafims a month of *ordinaria* which was assigned to him was not paid with regularity; and at the same time he expressed his regret that there was not shown to him the courtesy which was due to him. I strictly enjoined on you the good treatment which you should extend to him and the courtesy with which he should be respected, and that there should be no failure in paying what concerned him, nor in the increase of the further fifty xerafims a month which I ordered to be given him. And because it is in every way very convenient that this should be so carried out and fulfilled, I desire once again to command it to you, since the King of Candia, his brother, is showing himself gratified at what is done to him there.[30] Above all you must be on your guard that the Emperador should not go away from that city and that the Hollanders should not get him into their power for their own purposes, as they are designing.

I am ordering a reply to be sent to him to a letter of his in the form which seems to me suitable.

Written at Lisboa, the 31st of January, 1651.

The King.

(Doc. Rem. Livro 61 f. 418).

DOCUMENT 23

Domingos Rebello Lobo to the King.

The King of Ceilão who was lately converted and who is sustained here under the protection and royal shadow of your Majesty in this State, sent me the letter which I am forwarding herewith to be entrusted to your royal hand. I cannot refrain from laying bare to your Majesty the cruelty which is used towards this Prince since he left his lands and subjects. He is deprived of the *ordinaria* with which your Majesty was pleased to command that he should be assisted, when he ought to be greatly helped by V. R. R. for the devotion with which he set himself to accept the faith, and to look to the greatness of your Majesty to protect and restore him.

Throwing myself at your Majesty's feet I crave for pardon for the presumption on which I have ventured, trusting in my zeal for the royal service and on the obligation of the position which I hold, in the hope that God our Lord will turn his eyes of pity on this State which has cost the Portuguese so much, and on the royal Crown of Portugal, for the greater glory of him and of his holy faith.

May the Most High and Most Powerful God our Lord keep the most high and powerful person of your Majesty in his holy keeping, as I pray to him.

Goa, the 17th of January, 1649.

Domingos Rebello Lobo.[31]

(Doc. Rem. Liv. 61 f. 214, vo.)

DOCUMENT 24

Viceroy to King.

As soon as I received this letter of your Majesty, I am bidding the Secretary of State to go and visit the Emperador of Candia on our behalf and to convey to him what your Majesty was pleased to order in the same letter. In conformity therewith a *padrao* was at once issued to him for the allowance of fifty xerafims which your Majesty orders to be added to the 250, as is reported to your Majesty by another letter of this *Via*.

God protect, etc.

Goa, the 21st of December, 1651.

(Doc. Rem. Livro 61 f. 419).

NOTES.

1. For the connected negotiations and details of the Treaty, see Documentos Remettidos da India, Arquivo Nacional da Torre do Tombo, Lisbon, Livro 51, Ff 364-369.

2. Regarding the fortifying of Mata Kalapuwa and Trikona Malai, see Doc. Rem. Livro 12, Folio 4: King to Viceroy, 26th Feb., 1619.

L. 12, F. 5: Viceroy to King, Feb., 1620.
L. 15, F. 21: Viceroy to King, 20th Feb., 1621.
L. 16, F. 156: King to Viceroy, 9th Feb., 1622.
L. 17, F. 8 *vo*: Viceroy to King, 12th March, 1623.
L. 19, F. 15: Viceroy to King, Jan., 1624.
L. 19, F. 40 *vo*: Viceroy to King, Jan., 1624.
L. 20, F. 39: King to Viceroy, 24th Feb. 1624.
L. 21 F. 137: King to Viceroy, 13th Feb., 1625.
L. 22, F. 38 *v*: Viceroy to King, 4th Feb., 1625.
L. 22, F. 139: Viceroy to King, 25th Feb., 1626.
L. 23, F. 141: King to Viceroy, 7th March, 1626.
L. 24, F. 5 *v*: Viceroy to King, 13th Feb., 1627.
L. 25, F. 126: King to Viceroy, 10th April, 1628.
L. 26, F. 82: King to Viceroy, 24th Jan, 1629.
L. 27, F. 124: King to Viceroy, 26th March, 1630.

3. For the policy which led to the outbreak of hostilities and the incidents of the campaigns, see Doc. Rem. Livro 22, Folio 113: Viceroy to King, 2nd Feb., 1626.

L. 23, F. 141: King to Viceroy, 7th March, 1626.
L. 24, F. 14: Viceroy to King, Feb., 1627.
L. 25, F. 120: King to Viceroy, 22nd March, 1626.
L. 27, F. 86: King to Viceroy, 25th Feb., 1630.
L. 28, F. 16: King to Viceroy, 3rd Nov., 1631.
L. 28, F. 146: King to Viceroy, 31st Feb., 1631.
L. 29, F. 5: Viceroy to King, 5th March, 1631.
L. 29, F. 37: Viceroy to King, 5th Aug., 1631.
L. 29, F. 125: Viceroy to King, 22nd Sept., 1631.
L. 29, F. 139: Viceroy to King, 17th Dec., 1631.
L. 30, F. 158: King to Viceroy, 3rd April, 1632.
L. 30, F. 158: Viceroy to King, 12th Jan., 1633.

Interesting contemporary accounts of de Saa's overthrow are contained in two Mss. at the Biblioteca da Ajuda. One is entitled Rellatoria de Triste Suceco que teve a Conquista da Ilha de Ceilão, Codice 51-viii-40-peca 17, ff 188-199. The other is Jornada do Reino de Huva por Constantino de Saa de Noronha. Codice 51. iv.32; 72 folios. At my suggestion copies of these have been secured for the local Archives.

4. See Doc. Rem. Livro 30, F. 264 *v*: Viceroy to King, 4th Feb., 1633.

L. 31, F. 199: King to Viceroy, 8th March, 1634.

L. 37, F. 1: King to Viceroy, 28th Jan., 1636.

5. The Viceroy Dom Affonco to the King of Portugal, 27th June, 1552. Corpo Chronologico Parte 1, Maço 87, Doc. 73, Torre do Tombo: Translated in "Ceylon and Portugal; King and Christians."

6. Doc. Rem. Livro 40, F. 233: Viceroy to King, 31st December, 1637.

L. 42, F. 58: Viceroy to King, 27th Feb., 1638.

L. 43, F. 176: Captain General to Viceroy, Colombo, 22nd Dec., 1637.

L. 43, F. 179: Manuel Pinto to Captain General, Baticolo, 2nd Nov., 1637.

L. 43, F. 181: Cipher message from Padre Frey Christouão de Madre de Deos, at Kandy, to the Portuguese *arrayal*.

7. Doc. Rem. L. 41, F. 7 *vo*: Viceroy to King, 29th August, 1638.

L. 42, F. 58: Viceroy to King, 27th March, 1638.

L. 43, F. 177: Captain-General to Viceroy, 5th March, 1638.

L. 43, F. 185: Camara of Colombo to King, 17th April, 1638.

L. 43, F. 187: Camara to Captain General, 10th March, 1638.

L. 43, F. 187 *v*: Captain-General to Camara, 13th March, 1638.

L. 43, F. 188: Resolution of Camara, 8th March, 1638.

L. 46, F. 151: King to Viceroy, 6th May, 1639.

L. 46, F. 197: Viceroy to King, 27th July, 1641.

8. Doc. Rem. Livro 41, F. 55 *v*: Viceroy to King, 27th Sept., 1638.

9. In Antony Caen's Diary, under date the 17th of April, 1639, there is the entry of the receipt of a letter with the information that the King and his brother were reconciled. (Hague Archives: India Office Translations).

10. Translated in Ceylon Literary Register, Vol. ii. p. 367.

11. Captain João Ribeiro, who probably witnessed his reception, has left a vivid account of the incident. See his Fatalidade Historica da Ilha de Ceilão. Livro ii. Cap. 10 (Lisboa, 1836).

12. See Resolutions and Sentences of the Council of the Town of Galle, 11th Feb., 1642. Trans. in Journal R. A. S. (Ceylon) xvii., p. 299. He arrived in October, *ibid* xxx p. 128.

13 The date of Vijayapala's arrival at Goa is established by a letter written by Pieter Boreel, on the 29th of April, 1643, to the Governor-General at Batavia, Van Diemen. He himself arrived there on the 1st of April and he stated that the Prince reached there five days before with twenty Sinhalese, as the Portuguese had removed him from Colombo because they were afraid of his joining Raja Sinha or the Hollanders. He added "They do not think much of his intelligence and it is very probable he will not live long after turning Christian ; but the Portuguese will take care that before his death he shall make th m his heirs."

(Hague Archives : India Office Translations).

Martin Vinck who accompanied Boreel from Batavia, also wrote to the Governor-General, on the 25th of June, 1643, to convey the same news, as well as the rumour that the Prince had offered to turn Christian if made King of Ceylon, but that the Portuguese thought him wanting in mental capacity. Also see Doc. Rem. Livro 51, F. 242 : 3rd May, 1643.

14. This rare pamphlet was traced out at the Biblioteca of Evora owing to the persistence of Fraulein Fitzler.

15. Doc. Rem. L. 60, F. 394.

16. Translated by D. W. Ferguson Journal R. A. S. (Ceylon) xxi, 263.

17. Ribeiro, translation p. 141.

18. R. A. S. xxi. 260.

19. Duqueza da Mantua, grand-daughter of Philippe ii, who was selected as Queen Regent of Portugal, 1635-1641.

20. This is from a translation among the India Office Records. Another translation will be found printed in Ceylon Literary Register, ii, 69.

21. India Office Translations.

22. Same form of the word 'Bandara' is hidden behind this word. The description 'grand-daughter' is vaguely used, in the Sinhalese sense of a relation in the second generation.

23. Apparently palanquins or andoru.

24. For the importance attached to music as a mark of dignity, see the Gampola Perahera Case (D. C. Kandy No. 22, 466 which was taken in appeal before the Privy Council.

25. This son, and pretenders who claimed to be he, figure in the later dealings of Raja Sinha. See Ceylon and the Hollanders, Chapter ii.

26. A *Kurulla bendi male*. Ribeiro speaks of the wonderful catseye with nine *betas* or lines of light which the Prince wore on his arm at his arrival among the Portuguese (Trans. p. 72).

27. The Prince Dom João, who went to Portugal and built a church at Telheiras. For further particulars see "The Portuguese Era." The Church is now in a ruinous condition, and the marble slab with the Founder's arms has recently been removed to the Museo Carmo, thanks largely to the exertions of Fraulein Fitzler. The Prince's portrait, which was at the Biblioteca Nacional, has been destroyed as of no artistic value I was informed on inquiry there.

28. That is, King Dharmapala; he is called grandfather, according to the Sinhalese custom, as he married the Prince's grandfather Jaya Vira's sister.

29. The Spanish usurpation 1580-1640.

30. There is a Dutch report of 31st December, 1649, that Raja Sinha was detaining the Portuguese ambassador, as security for the safety of Vijaya Pala (India Office Translations)

31. For a valuable report by him on the state of Christianity in India, dated 17th Jan., 1649. See Doc. Rem. L, 61, Ff. 211-213 *v*.